FLIGHT

Written by Rob Alcraft

TOP THAT! Kids™

Copyright © 2004 Top That! Publishing plc
Tide Mill Way, Woodbridge, Suffolk, IP12 1AP, UK www.topthatpublishing.com
Top That! is a Registered Trademark of Top That! Publishing plc

Contents

For thousands of years, flying for humans was an impossible dream. However, this did not stop people from trying to fly. They would jump from cliffs and towers with little more than boards or feathers strapped to their bodies.

First Powered Flight

In 1903, the Wright Brothers made the first powered flight, a hop of just twelve seconds. Aircraft developed quickly and soon they were crossing the English Channel and then the Atlantic.

Modern Aircraft

Today there are aircraft that can fly to the edge of space, and others that can carry 360 tonnes of cargo. There are passenger airliners that can transport hundreds of people across thousands of miles of empty ocean.

Journeys that once would have taken months, now take hours. Flight has made our world seem smaller. We are connected now to more places, and more people, more quickly. Flying is a dream come true.

Aircraft have come a long way since the first attempts at flight. Today's state-of-the-art aircraft, like this Eurofighter, are far removed from the flimsy wood-and-fabric machines of only 100 years ago.

The Dream of Flying

The first people to try to fly thought they had to copy birds. They built incredible flapping machines or jumped from buildings holding bird wings. Others experimented with kites and gliders.

Death Leaps

Nearly 1,000 years ago, a man known as the Saracen of Constantinople jumped from a tower wearing a stiff cloak he thought would help him fly. He didn't. In 1874, Vincent De Groof had himself dropped from a balloon in a flapping ornithopter machine. He plunged to his death. There were many such birdmen. They all failed.

Model Flight

The first real flying machines were toys. Toy helicopters – really propellers on sticks – were being made and flown in China and Europe in the 1500s. Then, in 1871, a Frenchman called Pénaud built a model aircraft that could actually fly. The model had a propeller powered by a wound rubber band.

Balloons

In 1783, two men flew five miles across Paris in a balloon. It was the first human flight.

Belgian shoemaker Vincent de Groof jumped to his death in an attempt to fly.

The First Aviator

Otto Lilienthal of Germany was one of the most important pioneers of flight. He understood that gliding, not flapping, was the way to get airborne.

Dangerous

From 1891, he made over 1,000 flights on gliders he had designed and built himself. On August 9th, 1896, Lilienthal crashed while flying. He died from his injuries the next day.

Next Stage

Octave Chanute's glider experiments at Miller Beach, Indiana in 1896 produced the most important glider before the Wright brothers.

Otto Lilienthal glides through the air.

An Octave Chanute glider.

Even today, birdmen try the impossible!

The biggest leap forward for early aircraft was the invention of the internal combustion engine in 1885. The new engines were light and powerful. Suddenly, the lumbering weight of steam engines no longer held aircraft firmly on the ground.

Orville Wright's plane, Flyer 1.

The First Flight

The Wright brothers were the first to build aircraft that could really fly. Their first flight on 17th December, 1903 was just a hop of twelve seconds. However, they were soon making flights of more than 30 minutes. The Wright brothers had experimented with gliders for years. They understood how to make an aircraft stable, and how to control it.

Crossing the Channel

Aircraft improved quickly after the Wright brothers had shown what could be done. In 1909, Louis Blériot succeeded in crossing the English Channel.

Air War

In World War One, from 1914 to 1918, aircraft were used for spying, fighting and bombing. Aircraft design improved. They became stronger and flew faster. The Sopwith Camel, for example, could fly at 169 km/h (105 mph) and climb to a height of 20,000 feet.

Louis Blériot lands after crossing the English Channel.

A Sopwith Camel.

increasingly larger. The huge Short Sarafand flying boat could stay in the air for eleven hours. It didn't need an airport, but landed on water. There weren't many airports in existence at the time.

From Wood to Metal

By the 1930s, the wooden struts and double wings of the early biplanes had gone. Most aircraft were now built of metal. This made them stronger and faster Some, like the Supermarine S6B, could fly at over 644 km/h (400 mph).

The Boeing 247 was the first modern passenger aircraft.

Flying Boats

After World War One, the planes that people built became

Carrying Passengers

Aircraft were the quickest way to travel, and soon began to carry passengers and cargo. The Boeing 247 of 1933 was the first modern passenger airliner. It had a smooth, all-metal body, and could retract its undercarriage up into the body to reduce drag (the resistance caused by the air).

The Supermarine S6B could fly at over 575 km/h (370 mph).

The way in which a bird's wing moves is very complicated, and requires huge muscle strength. No person would ever be strong enough to fly like a bird. Aeroplane designers have, however, learned to duplicate the effect of a bird's wing.

The Wing

When a wing moves though the air, its shape creates upwards lift. This shape – with a curved top surface to the wing – is called an aerofoil. The lift it creates is the secret of flight. Lift on wings works the same for everything from jumbo jets to paragliders – and birds.

The 1893 Phillips multi-plane, which had many long, straight wings. It never flew.

What Wing Shape?

A wing's shape as viewed from above is called its planform.

Aircraft have different planform shapes, depending on their speed. Pilots can even alter the planform shape of some aircraft in flight.

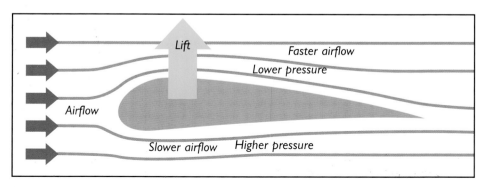

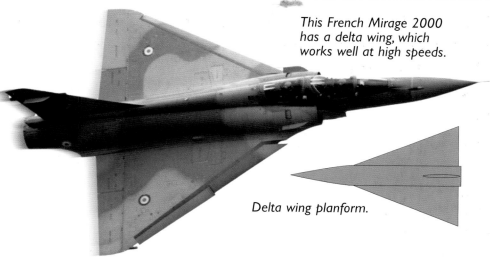

This French Mirage 2000 has a delta wing, which works well at high speeds.

Delta wing planform.

Delta

Delta wings are named after the Greek letter delta, which looks like a triangle. This kind of wing works well at high speeds, but requires longer runways for take-off and landing.

Long and Straight

Long, straight wings work better at low speeds. Gliders and light, powered aircraft have this kind of wing.

Glider wing planform.

Gliders have long, straight wings which work better at low speeds.

Staying in the Air

Bicycles and cars can only turn left or right, but flying is very different. A plane flies in three dimensions. It can go left or right like a car, but it can also go up and down, and it can tip from side to side. A pilot has to use the following three sets of controls at the same time.

Yaw

Pilots can move the rudder pedals with their feet, making the plane go left and right with the rudder.

Roll

Moving the control stick side to side moves the ailerons, which tip the plane's wings one way or the other.

Pitch

The control stick also moves the elevators. Pushing the stick forward sends the plane heading down. Pulling it back points the plane up.

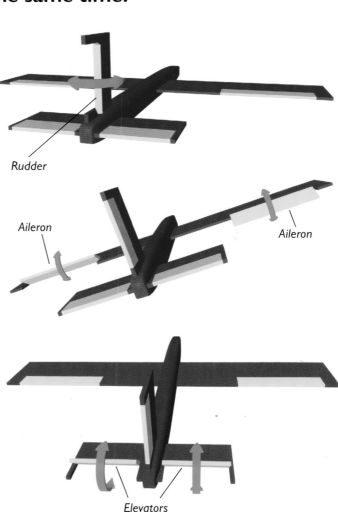

Rudder

Aileron

Aileron

Elevators

Air Speed

Speed is essential for flight. An aircraft's wings have to move through the air to create lift. If an aircraft goes too slowly, it will stall. Different aircraft fly at different speeds. A hang-glider can fly at just 24 km/h (15 mph) because it is very light. An airliner weighs many tonnes and will fall out of the air if it goes much slower than 240 km/h (150 mph).

Drag

As an aircraft flies, it has to push air out of

Streamlined aircraft like this F16 fighter have smooth shapes.

the way. Things that stick out make this more difficult – it would be like trying to run fast while holding a big board flat in front of you. This is called

drag. To help aircraft fly well, designers streamline them in order to cut down the drag. This makes the aircraft faster and more efficient.

Formation aerobatic flying requires great skill and precision.

From the biggest to the fastest, these are some amazing unexpected machines which have managed to fly – and some which haven't.

The Widest
At 97 m, the 1947 Hercules flying boat has the longest wingspan of any plane. Built entirely from wood, it was nicknamed the Spruce Goose. It flew once.

The Sky Baby biplane is tiny!

One Small Hop
The Wright brothers first flight lasted for just 37 m.

Short and Sweet
The Sky Baby is the plane with the world's shortest wingspan – just 1.67 m.

The Spruce Goose is now on display in California.

Flying Sheep
The first living things to fly in a balloon were a sheep, a chicken and a duck. They made their flight in 1782. The animals were used as test pilots, to see if there was enough air to breathe high above the ground.

Bullet Power
In 1870 a Frenchman, Gustave Trouvé, built a flying model ornithopter. It was

powered by bullets!
Blank cartridges would
fire though tubes,
forcing wings to flap.
Amazingly, Trouvé's
ornithopter flew
over 70 m.

Powered Hops

By the 1890s,
inventors across the
world were making
the first powered
hops. In France, a
steam-powered
aircraft with wings like
a bat made a short
hop in 1890.

The Frost Ornithopter, a machine which flapped but didn't fly.

Clement Ader's 'Eole', which was yet another failed ornithopter.

① Amazing Feats

Daring has always been a necessary part of flying. Early pilots often risked their lives to earn a living and to prove what aircraft could do.

Stunt Women

The 1920s was the age of the flying circus. Pilots and planes toured America and Europe, doing stunts and displays in front of paying crowds. It was women who often did the daring, crazy stunts – including wing walking. There were no nets or safety harnesses. If you fell off, you died.

Lillian Boyer, a famous 'barnstormer' of the 1920s.

First Across the Atlantic

In 1919, two pilots, John Alcock and Arthur Brown, made the first non-stop flight across the Atlantic. Their plane was a converted World War One bomber called a Vickers Vimy.

Record Breaker

The fastest aircraft in the world is the rocket-powered X15. It can fly at 7,274 km/h (4,520 mph), more than 300 times the speed of the Wright brothers' first flight, and six times the speed of sound.

A Vickers Vimy like this one made the world's first non-stop transatlantic crossing.

Faster than a Bullet

The Space Shuttle orbits Earth at 8 km (5 miles) per second – more than ten times faster than the speed of a bullet.

Nose Cone

Concorde grows up to 25 cm (10 in) longer in supersonic flight. High-speed air friction makes its metal body expand – and so it gets longer.

The Lowest Flying Aircraft

Hovercraft are the lowest flying aircraft. They fly along on a cushion of air, held in by big rubber skirts.

Pedal Power

In 1962, the dream of human-powered flight came true. The balsa wood

The Gossamer Albatross flew 36 km (22 miles) across the English Channel.

Puffin made the first straight-line flight over half a mile. In 1979, another pedal-powered aircraft called the Gossamer Albatross flew across the English Channel.

A modern hovercraft.

The world's heaviest aircraft is the Russian-built Antonov An-225. It weighs 600 tonnes and was built to carry a Russian space shuttle.

Aircraft carry millions of passengers every year – travelling billions of miles between them. Today air travel is easy, but in the early days it was uncomfortable and dangerous.

The First Passenger Aircraft Leftovers

After World War One, there were lots of aircraft and pilots with nothing to do. In the USA, a mail service started using old bombers. In Europe, an air service was started between London and Paris. The flight took over 2 1/2 hours and passengers were given hot water bottles to keep them warm.

One of the first passengers aboard the Wright Flyer.

The Junkers F13 first flew in 1919.

Zeppelins were popular in the 1920s.

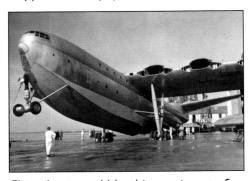

Flying boats could land in exotic, out-of-the-way places.

Junkers F13

The 1919 Junkers F13 was the world's first purpose-built airliner. It was incredibly reliable, and many were still flying safely twenty years later.

A Handley Page 42 in the 1920s.

Giants of the Air

In the 1920s, airships were the really luxurious way to travel. The Graf Zeppelins – filled with hydrogen to keep them in the air – carried passengers across the Atlantic. The giant *Hindenburg* airship was 245 m (800 ft) long, and would have made a modern jumbo jet look small. Unfortunately, the *Hindenburg* exploded into flames in 1937, and airships lost their popularity.

Flying Boats

Flying boats began inter-continental travel. At the time, there were few airports, but these planes could land in many places. Planes like the Latecoere were big. It set the longest sea plane flight record at 5,763 km (3,581 miles) from Morocco to Brazil.

Handley Page 42

The Handley Page 42 was an old-style airliner, that flew up to 38 passengers in luxury. It flew over 2 million miles without a fatal crash.

Dakota

One of the most successful airliners is the Douglas DC 3 – or Dakota. It first flew in 1935, and was reliable and quick. Over 10,000 were built, and many are still flying today.

DC3s are still flying today.

The age of air travel really took off after World War Two. The lessons learned from bomber aircraft, and the invention of the jet engine, made fast, smooth air travel possible. The more powerful the new jet engines were, the bigger the planes could be.

Go Large

The largest airliner flying today is the Boeing 747, otherwise known as the Jumbo Jet. It weighs over 450 tons and stands more than twice the height of a house. It has a range of 10,988 km (6,828 miles), and has sixteen toilets and six galleys. The 747 is designed for long-haul flying, from one continent to another. They often fly from Europe to Australia.

This French Falcon 900 carries nineteen passengers.

Go Small

Not all modern passenger aircraft are huge. Small passenger jets are often owned by companies or rich individuals.

This Boeing 747 is operated by Australian airline Qantas.

Inside an Airliner

Today's airliners have pressurised passenger cabins. Inside the plane, people can breathe normal air and keep warm. Outside, the air is very thin and freezing cold. Aircraft built with pressurised cabins can fly above the weather, and give a smooth, comfortable ride. The first passenger planes had to fly through the weather, and air travel was very bumpy.

The Nuisance of Noise Pollution

Although air travel is very popular, people do not like flight paths to pass over their houses. Nor do they like airports to be built near their homes. The noise pollution can be disruptive, and traffic also builds up in the area as cars travel to and from the airport.

Many airports are located near residential areas.

Modern airliners are comfortable.

Combat Aircraft

When World War One started in 1914, aircraft were used only as spy planes. Their job was to spot troop movements and artillery targets. Aircraft combat started with pilots shooting at each other with hunting rifles, or dropping hand-held bombs.

First Fighter

The Vicker's Gunbus was the first specialised fighter aircraft, and flew from 1915. A gunner would sit in the front seat, with the pilot behind. It would take the Gunbus half an hour to reach its maximum flying height of 9,000 feet.

The gunner in this Gunbus sat in the front seat.

Deadly Weapon

The Fokker E.III was a single-wing fighter, or monoplane. It was the first aircraft fitted with an interrupter gear which let the pilot fire forwards through the propeller. For about three months in 1915/1916, the E.III was the most deadly aircraft in the sky.

A German E.III.

Strong and Reliable

The SE 5a was a strong and reliable fighter plane, with a forward firing gun. Some were fitted with bomb racks to carry four 25 lb bombs. After the war, the 50 SE 5a was used as the first skywriting aircraft.

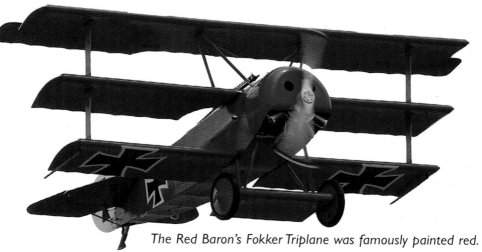

The Red Baron's Fokker Triplane was famously painted red.

Red Baron

The Fokker Triplane had triple wings. It was famous as the plane of Manfred von Richthofen – the Red Baron. He shot down 20 of his 80 kills with a Fokker triplane, before being shot down himself in April 1918.

Short Careers

World War One fighter pilots flew in open cockpits. High above Earth, the cold, thin air would slow the engines and the pilots' reactions. The conditions often caused machine guns to jam. It was extremely dangerous. At times during the war, the life expectancy of a new pilot was just two months.

World War One pilots were daring and brave.

Fighter planes have always been the world's fastest and most advanced aircraft. Today's fighters can streak along at amazing speeds, and climb almost to the edge of space.

20,000 Spitfires were built.

First Jet Fighter

The Messerschmitt Me 262 was one of the first jet fighters. First used in 1944, it had a maximum speed of 871 km/h (541 mph) and could outrun any other

Massive Engine

The Spitfire was fast for its time, World War Two. Powered by a massive 1,554 horse power Merlin engine, it could make 575 km/h (357 mph), and could climb 5,000 feet in 1 minute 36 seconds.

The Flying Fortress had a crew of 10.

Mosquito

This bomber could fly at 657 km/h (408 mph), faster than any fighter, and still carry around a tonne of bombs.

Stay and Fight

The first Flying Fortress bomber appeared in battle in 1943. Unlike the Mosquito, the B17 did not try to outrun enemy aircraft – but fight them. It had a crew of ten, including five gunners. It could fly 3,220 km (2,000 miles) and carry nearly 3 tonnes of bombs.

fighter in the sky. It could also climb to a height of over 40,000 feet.

The Mosquito's frame was built entirely of wood.

Russian MiGs

MiG jet fighters are some of the most successful. The Russian-built planes, which first appeared in

The MiG 29 carries 'smart' weapons that can be guided onto their targets.

The Me 262 was the fastest fighter of World War Two.

1958, have been updated many times. The MiG 29 is very agile – it can practically stop in mid-air or shoot straight upwards.

Fastest

The fastest jet plane is the Blackbird. It can fly at 871 km/h (2,193 mph), over three times the speed of sound. Its weird shape and matt black colour are designed to make it invisible to radar. Its main job is to spy on the enemy.

Big Mover

Moving goods about is an important job for

modern armies – and aircraft. The American C5 Galaxy transport can carry more than 120 tonnes of anything, from tanks to other aircraft, for more than 3,500 miles.

The SR-71 Blackbird is the world's fastest jet plane.

The C5 Galaxy is huge!

Jet Power

Jet power changed flying for ever, enabling aircraft to fly faster and higher. In fact, weight for weight, a jet is more powerful than any other kind of aircraft engine. Just one Boeing 747 engine gives the same power as 50 cars.

How Jets Work
A jet's power comes from forcing a blast of burning air and gas backwards out of the engine. This blast of gas sends it shooting forward – just like the way a balloon will shoot forward if you blow it up and let it go.

Modern jet engines are complex and large.

Inside a Jet Engine
Big forces and temperatures are at work inside a jet engine. Special alloys and ceramics are used to make the engine's casing and moving parts – so they don't melt or break.

Compression
A jet engine sucks in air and squeezes it through a system of many layers of spinning fan blades. At this compression stage, some engines will compress the air 30 times over.

Combustion
Nozzles spray fuel into the engine, which burns at over 1,500°C (2,700°F). The air and gas in the engine are squeezed massively.

Thrust
The burning gas and air roar out of the engine – travelling at over 2,090 km/h (1,300 mph). This gives the engine its forward power – called thrust. As the gases rush out, they turn turbine blades, which drive the compressors at the front of the engine.

Maximum Power

Afterburners are rings of nozzles that spray burning fuel into the jet's exhaust. The burning fuel adds massive extra thrust – like adding the power of another half engine, but without any more weight. Afterburners get maximum power from a jet. Fighter planes use them in combat, or for short, high speed take-offs.

The afterburners on this jet fighter give it more thrust.

The First Jet Engine

The first working jet engine was built in 1937 in an old factory outside Rugby, in England. Its inventor, Frank Whittle, was a test pilot and engineer. His engine worked – but it often caught fire, and leaked fuel. It was four years before it ran well enough to power a jet airplane.

The Turbofan

Most passenger aircraft are fitted with turbofan jet engines. Turbofan engines have a fan at the front. The fan drags air through and around the engine, adding power and saving fuel.

Turbofan engines have many rows of fan blades.

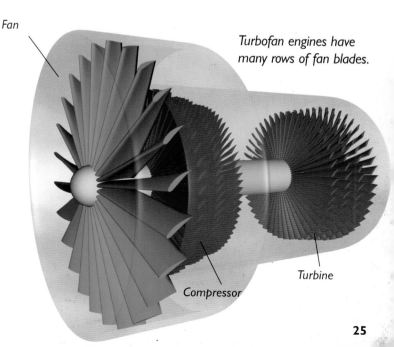

Fan

Compressor

Turbine

Supersonic Flight

People once believed that flying faster than sound – going supersonic – was impossible. When you think that the first flight was only 24 km/h (15 mph), it did seem unlikely. But then, in 1937, the jet engine was invented. Soon jet planes were flying close to the sound barrier.

Rocket Planes

The first plane to break the sound barrier was a rocket plane – the 1947 Bell X-1. It was piloted by U. S. Air Force pilot Chuck Yeager. Rockets work like jet engines, by blasting burning fuel backwards out of the engine. Unlike jets, rockets carry their own oxygen supply.

The first supersonic plane, the Bell X-1.

Speedy Travel

Concorde is the only passenger aircraft that can fly faster than sound. It cruises at over 2,090 km/h (1,300 mph) – and can travel from London to New York in three hours – half the time of a traditional passenger jet. Concorde also flies at over 26 km (16 miles) above Earth – twice the height of ordinary passenger aircraft. At this height, there isn't much air turbulence, and Concorde can fly faster and more smoothly.

G-force

When fighter jets turn or accelerate upwards, gravity pulls hard on the plane – and the pilot. This extra pulling force is called 'g' force. Pilots can experience a

Chuck Yeager.

lot of 'g',
and may black
out because the
blood can't pump
around their bodies.

Concorde made its first flight in 1969 and entered commercial service seven years later.

Inflatable Trousers
To help avoid this, jet
pilots wear an anti-g
suit, which have
inflatable pads that

force blood back up to
the pilot's heart and
brain, to stop them
blacking out.

This aerobatic pilot is showing the effects of negative 'g'
force, which forces blood to the head.

G-suits can help to stop pilots from blacking out during sharp turns.

Not all aircraft need runways for take-off. Some can take off and land vertically, anywhere – from the deck of a ship to a small patch of grass. These aircraft have some of the advantages of a helicopter, but remain as fast and deadly as a jet fighter.

The Flying Bedstead

The first vertical take-off aircraft was the sensibly named Thrust Measuring Rig – but it looked just like a bed frame, and everyone called it the Flying Bedstead. It made its first proper flight in 1954, using four engines pointing down to lift it into the air.

Up, Up and Away

Many very odd-looking vertical take-off aircraft were built. The French built the Coleoptére, which flew in 1959. Its giant round body and stumpy wings looked

The French Coleoptére.

like a comic book space craft. It crashed two months after its first flight.

Harrier Jump Jet

Using lessons learned from the Flying Bedstead, the Harrier Jump Jet became the first successful vertical take-off and landing aircraft. It made its first flight in 1961 – and versions of it are

The Flying Bedstead proved that jets could hover.

The Harrier is still in use today – more than 40 years since it first flew.

still in use today. It uses swivelling nozzles on its engine to give it up and forward thrust. Once in the air, it can fly at 1,064 km/h (661 mph). It is equipped with missiles, and 25 mm cannons that can fire thousands of shells a minute.

21st Century

The Lockheed Martin F-35 Joint Strike Fighter will be the world's first supersonic jet fighter with vertical take-off and landing capabilities.

The Joint Strike Fighter will be produced in three versions, including this hovering F-35B.

Fly-by-Wire

As aircraft have become faster, flying them has become more difficult. Pilot reaction time is now one of the main limitations on aircraft design. To help pilots, designers have created a new way of controlling aircraft – called fly-by-wire.

Out with the Old
Aircraft have always been controlled mechanically. That means there's a cable, or hydraulic pipe, connecting the pilot's controls to the control surfaces such as the rudder. It's not that different to the way a bike's brakes or gears are controlled by cables. Fly-by-wire technology gets rid of all these mechanical links and cables by using electrical circuits and computers.

The Electronic Pilot
Fly-by-wire was first tested in the air in 1972 in a U. S. F8 fighter jet. Fly-by-wire control is not limited by the speed of human reflexes. It enables aircraft – especially fighter jets – to be more responsive and aerobatic, because fly-by-wire will keep

Fly-by-wire technology makes modern aircraft more manoeuvrable, stable and safe.

The Joint Strike Fighter would not be able to fly without fly-by-wire technology.

the wings level where a human pilot might not be able to.

High-Speed Help

At high speed, flying surfaces such as ailerons are forced out of position, and keeping an aircraft stable is very difficult. Fly-by-wire adjusts the way an aircraft is flying automatically. A pilot can do something else, like target a weapon, while the aircraft flies itself. Without the computer, the aircraft would be unstable.

Idiot Proof

Fly-by-wire technology makes sure a pilot doesn't do the wrong thing, like pull too sharp a turn, or too steep a dive. Some aircraft even have a return to level button. If a pilot gets into trouble, this function will put the aeroplane back upright and flying safely.

In the F-16, the pilot moves the controls, and the computer then moves the control surfaces.

◑ Gliders

The first aircraft were gliders. Men like Percy Pilcher, who flew in the 1890s, made and flew some of the first working gliders. He would jump from hills to get airborne. Today's gliders are hi-tech flying machines made from fibreglass and the latest plastics.

Early Gliders

Many people believe that the first successful aeroplane glider was built in 1853 by Sir George Cayley. He employed his coachman to fly it.

Super Fliers

Modern gliders are very aerodynamic. Their smooth shapes cut through the air with very little to slow

Percy Pilcher's 1899 glider.

them down. They fly very efficiently – and can glide forward

100 metres, while only losing two metres of altitude.

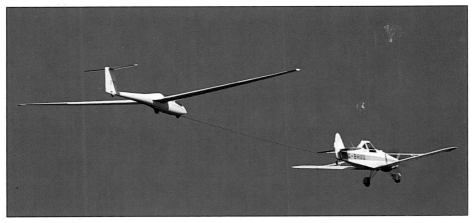

A glider being towed by another plane.

Some gliders have small engines which pilots switch off when they wish to glide.

Expert

In a glider, you can soar above Earth for hours. The secret is catching thermals, or rising currents of air, in the same way that surfers catch a wave.

Take-off

Gliders need help to get into the air. The cheapest and quickest way is a ground tow, from a winch or a car. Towing like this will get a glider to around 1,000 feet. A better way to get airborne is to have a tow from another plane. This way gliders can get up to 3,000 feet before they are on their own.

Solo Flight

Glider pilots need an average of 50 take-offs and landings with an instructor before they can fly solo.

Know your Stuff

You can train to fly gliders when you're only sixteen years old, but there's a lot to learn. Pilots need to know how the weather works, how to navigate across open country, and how to fly the glider safely. Learner pilots often fly slower, more stable machines.

Airbrakes

Gliders have brakes. These big flaps bang open to slow the glider as it lands.

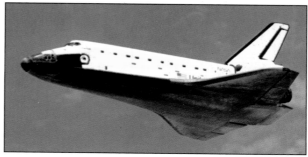

The Space Shuttle is probably the world's biggest glider!

Microlights are basic flying machines that are easy to fly and to look after. They can take off and land in a field, and fold up onto a trailer.

Take your Pick

There are two basic kinds of microlight, many of which can carry two people. Some look – and fly – like small aeroplanes. Others, often called trikes, are like a hang-glider with an engine. These trikes have simple open cockpits which hang underneath the wing.

A flexwing microlight taking off.

Some microlights look like flying sun loungers!

Power

The first microlights were just hang-gliders with engines attached. Some even used motorcycle engines. Today they use light, specially built engines. They carry enough fuel for about four hours flying, and cruise at around 48 km/h (30 mph).

Launch

Microlights don't need a lot of space for runways. Their take off speed is just 32 km/h (20 mph) – you can probably ride your bike that fast! When the machine reaches this speed, the pilot pushes forward on the control frame, and launches into the air.

Where To?

Microlight pilots plan their route before they take off, so they know where to land if they have a problem.

Rules

When microlights first flew, there were no rules and no training. Anyone could – and did – just build their own microlight and teach themselves to fly it. It was a bit like the very earliest days of flying, but with engines. This freedom was a big reason why many

A flexwing microlight touching down.

people took up the sport. Unfortunately, some early microlight pilots crashed and killed themselves, and today there are strict rules for building and flying microlights. Today you have to be seventeen years old before you can get a licence to fly.

This three-axis control microlight has conventional aircraft controls.

Helicopter flight was the first flight imagined by humans. Ancient Chinese children played with a hand-spun toy that, when revolved rapidly, rose upward.

Early Inventor

The Italian inventor, Leonardo da Vinci, made drawings of a machine that looked remarkably like a helicopter 500 years ago. His design, like many others to follow, would work in theory, but could not have actually flown, had it been possible to make it at the time. All early models lacked a true understanding of the nature of lift and an adequate engine.

Modern helicopters are fast and safe.

Problems Solved

Once the internal combustion engine had been developed, it provided a suitable power source. Engineers then had to experiment with an engine fitted to allow a rotor to force the fuselage to rotate in the opposite direction to the engine.

Off the Ground

On 13th November, 1907, a French man named Paul Cornu lifted a twin-rotored helicopter into the air (entirely without assistance from the ground) for a few seconds. This was probably the world's first helicopter flight.

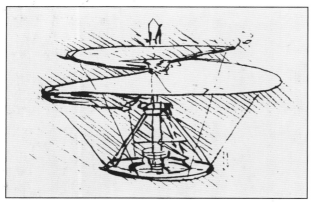

Leonardo da Vinci envisaged the helicopter hundreds of years ago.

Invaluable

Nowadays, helicopters are one of the most versatile and important vehicles in the world. They are used to transport people to various locations which are difficult to reach with other vehicles, such as oil rigs, for aerial photography, for delivering mail to remote areas and for to monitor the traffic on busy roads and to assist in the capture of criminals.

Military Helicopters

The military use helicopters to carry equipment and troops, as assault aircraft, as gun ships, as antisubmarine aircraft, for electronic warfare and for humanitarian missions.

Helicopters can help to put out forest fires.

No Wings!

Gyrocopters have rotor arms instead of wings. These rotors might look like a helicopter's, but they're not powered by an engine. Instead, they spin as the gyrocopter moves through the air. Each rotor arm is shaped like a wing. As they spin they act like wings, to give the gyrocopter lift.

A military rescue helicopter.

several uses on large farms. They are used by emergency services to transport injured people to hospital, as search and rescue vehicles, to help extinguish forest fires,

A 1930s Cierva gyrocopter.

Hang-gliding is as close as you can get to soaring like a bird. Pilots have to leap from hills or cliffs to get into the air. Once airborne, hang-glider pilots catch wind and rising air that can carry them higher and keep them flying.

Flying Wings

Hang gliders are simple flying wings. They can be put together – rigged – in around ten minutes. They are made from tough nylon material, stretched over a frame made from aluminium tubes, and held taut by steel wires. They weigh about 28 kg. The first modern versions were built by the U. S. space agency NASA, who designed

Hang-gliders are made from tough nylon.

them to help land space capsules.

Getting into the Air

Hang-gliders have no engine. To get airborne, hang-glider pilots have to use hills and cliffs. They lift the glider and run downhill, into the wind.

Harness

The pilots hang in a harness that looks a bit like a sleeping bag. This harness has pockets to keep maps and a small two-way radio, and keeps the pilot warm and comfortable. Pilots also carry a variometer which tells

Hang-glider pilots hang in a harness.

them how fast they are rising or falling. This is important information, because in the air, it's sometimes hard to tell if you're going up or down.

Control

To control and steer a hang-glider, the pilot uses the weight of their body. For instance, if they pull on the control bar, and shift their body forward the glider will descend and speed up. If they move their body to the right the glider will turn right.

Staying in the Air

Once in the air, there are two ways a hang-

Pilots use their body to direct the hang-glider.

Up with the birds!

glider pilot can stay flying. One method is to catch thermals, which are currents of warm air rising from the ground. If they circle in these, they will gain height. The other way is to use hill lift – where wind coming up against a hill will rise and go over it. Pilots can fly back and forth along a hill using this rising air to stay flying. The longest flight ever is 36 hours.

Paragliding and Paramotoring

Paragliding is one of the simplest kinds of flying. The paraglider pilot hangs underneath a large flexible wing. If a pilot can catch wind from hills and rising patches of warm air, they can stay flying for hours. The distance record for paragliding is 336 km (209 miles), set in South Africa in 1995.

A Paraglider Wing

The paraglider wing is made of tough, light nylon. It has lots of compartments that inflate as air passes through them. This gives the paraglider the shape of a wing and provides lift.

Paragliding pilots use brakes to control direction.

Gliding down a mountain.

Jumping off Mountains

Paragliding began when new, steerable parachutes were invented in the 1960s. People had the idea of using them to glide down mountains. The mountains had to be high and steep, so only people living in the Alps could fly the first paragliders.

Paragliding and Paramotoring

Paramotor engines form part of the harness.

The First Jump

Paragliders are based on parachutes which are, along with balloons, the oldest way of flying. The first parachute jump was in 1783. A man called Louis Lenormand jumped from a tree, and landed successfully. Modern paragliders are based on the same idea, but are a lot more advanced. Today's paraglider wings weigh only 4 kilos.

Brake Control

Unlike any other kind of aircraft, paragliders are controlled by brakes. The brakes are two set of control lines attached to the wing. By pulling on one brake line, the pilot can steer the paraglider left or right.

Paramotoring

Some paragliders have engines. This is called paramotoring. A paramotoring pilot actually wears their aircraft engine with their harness. Engines can weigh as little as 17 kg. Paraglider pilots can fly at around 40 km/h (25 mph) and stay in the air for around two hours.

Paragliding is based on parachuting.

The Space Shuttle

The Space Shuttle is part rocket-powered space ship, part glider. It is the world's first aircraft that can fly to space, and back again.

Lots of Bits
Each Shuttle aircraft is made from over 600,000 different parts. Over 15,000 people are needed to prepare each Shuttle mission for space.

Countdown
The Shuttle's countdown to lift-off is 3 1/2 days long.

Lift-off
The Shuttle's five main engines ignite, and the shuttle blasts away from Earth. Two minutes after lift-off, the Shuttle is already 41 km (25 miles) above Earth.

Back to Earth
Its two long rocket engines – or boosters – are empty and have done their job. They fall away back to Earth.

3... 2... 1... lift-off!

Fast Escape
The Shuttle must reach a speed of around 45,000 km/h (28,000 mph) to escape Earth's gravity. After eight minutes, the Shuttle has left Earth's atmosphere. The main fuel tank then falls away and burns up.

Preparing for lift-off.

Walking in space.

More Bits
Once in space, the Shuttle has 44 small rocket engines that help it to manoeuvre. On the flight deck, there are over 2,100 switches!

Take a Walk
Space walks are part of many missions. Astronauts leave the shuttle in special suits to do their work. The conditions are extreme. The side of the suit facing the Sun may reach 150°C, while the dark side can be around −129°C.

Coming Home
The Shuttle re-enters Earth's atmosphere at 25 times the speed of sound. The friction of air rubbing against the Shuttle heats its skin until it glows red hot. To protect it from the heat, the Shuttle is covered in 34,000 special heat-resistant tiles.

Touchdown!

Opening the cargo doors.

Big Glider
The Shuttle glides down through Earth's atmosphere. When it

lands, the Shuttle is still going around 350km/h (215 mph), and needs 2.5 km (1.5 miles) of runway to stop.

A parachute helps the Shuttle to slow down.

Only 100 years ago, aircraft were flying at just 24 km/h (15 mph). Planes were built of wood and cloth, and a half-hour flight was amazing. Today, aircraft of 600 tonnes can heave themselves into the air. If things have changed this much, think what aircraft could be like in the future!

Smarter?

The Eurofighter will use the latest computer technology. Pilots will be able to choose targets just by looking at them. The plane will be programmed to talk – giving pilots warnings and information.

A vision of the future – the Eurofighter.

Higher?

Perhaps space flight will become even easier. The American X-33 was one idea for an Earth to Space aircraft – but it was too expensive to build.

Another idea was the Horizontal Take Off and Landing (HOTOL) aircraft. The HOTOL was to have rocket engines that didn't need heavy tanks of oxygen. However, this aircraft has also proved too expensive to build.

The X-33 proved too expensive.

The A380 will carry 800 people.

Bigger?

Passenger aircraft are getting bigger. The Airbus A380 is designed to carry over 800 people. Flights like this will mean a lot of people can fly a long way at a low cost.

Smaller?

Bigger is not always better. Some airline companies are betting on small aircraft. These will take people to small airports close to where they actually want to be.

Just Different

Aircraft like the Boeing V-22 Osprey are flying now. It can tilt its propellers and take off vertically. It then rotates its propellers forward for high-speed flight. Perhaps aircraft of the future will seem as unusual as this one.

The Boeing V-22 Osprey.

ⓘ Glossary

Aerobatics Aircraft stunts.

Aerodynamic A smooth shape that cuts easily through the air.

Aerofoil The special shape of an aircraft wing, curved on top, and flat on the bottom. As it moves through the air it produces upwards lift.

Ailerons Moving surfaces on an aircraft's wings. Pilots use the ailerons to roll a plane left or right.

Air turbulence Bumps and jumps caused by moving air.

Airliner An aircraft built to carry lots of people.

Airship A powered, cigar-shaped balloon that carries passengers.

Aluminium A metal used to make aircraft because it is very light.

Biplane An aircraft with two sets of wings.

Cargo A load that needs to be carried.

Ceramic Non-metal materials made by firing in a kiln the way clay is made into pottery.

F117 Stealth Fighter.

Cockpit The place where a pilot sits.

Composites Modern materials that are light and strong.

Control frame An A-shaped frame on a hang-glider or microlight.

Control surfaces An aircraft's moving flaps such as the rudder.

Design How something should look and work.

Drag The slowing force on an aircraft as it pushes through the air.

Elevators The moving surfaces on an aircraft's wings. A pilot uses the elevators to climb or dive.

Flying boat An aircraft with floats instead of wheels.

G force The force that pulls down on a

pilot as they accelerate away from Earth, or make a sharp turn.

Galley The name for a kitchen in a boat or aircraft.

Glass fibre Also called fibeglass. A strong and easily shaped material, often usedin gliders, that is also light.

Glider An aircraft with no engine.

Gravity The pull of Earth, the force that keeps our feet on the ground, and makes apples fall.

Gyrocopter A propeller-driven aircraft with rotor blades instead of wings.

Harness The straps and gear which hold a pilot safely in place.

Helicopter An aircraft with a spinning rotor, instead of wings.

Horsepower A measurement of an engine's power. Many of today's cars have engines of around 100 horse power.

Internal combustion engine An engine which burns gas. The burning fuel forces pistons up and down, which turns wheels and gears.

Interrupter gear A way of making sure a machine gun does not fire into an aircraft's propeller.

Jet engine Works by squeezing and burning gas and air and forcing these to explode out of the back of the jet engine. This make forward thrust.

NASA National Aeronautics and Space Administration, set up by the American government to experiment with flight and space travel.

Navigate Find your way around.

Orbit The loop around Earth travelled by a satellite, space craft or other object in space.

Ornithopter Invented name for early flying machines that had flapping wings.

Oxygen A gas that people need to breathe, and which is also needed to make things burn.

Paraglider A kind of flying which uses a large wing – a bit like a parachute.

Pressurised Air pressure is highest on the ground, and much lower high in the air. An aircraft which is pressurised keeps the same air pressure no matter how high the aircraft goes. This keeps the passengers comfortable.

Glossary

Propeller A spinning blade that can pull or push an aircraft through the air.

Rocket engine An engine that works like a jet engine. It squeezes and burns gas, forcing it backwards out of the engine to create forward thrust. A rocket carries oxygen and does not burn air. Rockets can work in space.

Rudder A moving flap on the tail of an aircraft that helps the pilot turn an aircraft left or right.

Soaring Gliding high in the air.

Solo Flying alone, without an instructor.

Stall When a plane flies too slowly, it drops quickly into a downward dive.

Steam engine or steam power An engine that uses steam to force a piston up and down, and turn wheels and gears.

Strut A support or bar added for strength.

Supersonic Travelling faster than the speed of sound.

Thermal A name for a rising patch of warm air.

Thrust A pushing force.

Turbine A turbine is a set of spinning blades. Turbines work like a windmill.

Smart weapon A name for rockets and missiles that can follow and choose targets to blow up.

Key: top - t; middle - m; bottom - b; left - l; right - r;
APL - Aviation Picture Library (www.aviationpictures.com)

Front Cover: (l, r) Corel; (m) Digital Vision. Back Cover: Corel. 1: Digital Vision. 2/3: EADS/APL. 4: Getty Images. 5: (t) APL; (m) Philip Jarrett; (b) Getty Images. 6: (t) Getty Images; (b) John Stroud Collection/APL. 7: (t) Getty Images; (m, b) John Stroud Collection/APL. 8: (t) Philip Jarrett; (b) TTAT. 9: (t, b) Corel; (m) TTAT. 10: TTAT. 11: Corel. 12: Austin J. Brown/APL. 13: (t) Philip Jarrett; (b) APL. 14: (t) Getty Images; (b) Corel. 15: (t) Getty Images; (m) Flat Earth; (b) Corel. 16: (t) APL; (b) Philip Jarrett; (bl) APL/QPL; (br) Getty Images. 17: (t) John Stroud Collection/APL; (b) Corel. 18: (t) Francois Robineau-Dassault/APL; (b) Austin J. Brown/APL. 19: (t) Austin J. Brown/APL; (b) APL/Airbus. 20: (t) John Stroud Collection/APL; (b) Getty Images. 21: (t) Corel; (b) Philip Jarrett. 22: (t) Austin J. Brown/APL; (m,b) 23: (t, b) Corel; (ml) Getty Images; (mr) Digital Vision. 24: APL/General Electric. 25: (t) Corel; (b) TTAT. 26: Getty Images. 27: Austin J. Brown/APL; (b) Philip Jarrett. 28: (t) Philip Jarrett; (b) Getty Images. 29: (t) Austin J. Brown/APL; (b) Lockheed Martin Aeronautics Company. 30: Digital Vision. 31: (t) Lockheed Martin Aeronautics Company; (b) Corel. 32: (t) Getty Images; (b) Austin J. Brown/APL. 33: (t) Austin J. Brown/APL; (b) Corel. 34: (t) Corel; (b) Airsport Photo Library. 35: (t) Austin J. Brown/APL; (b) Airsport Photo Library. 36: (t) Corel; (b) Philip Jarrett. 37: (t) Austin J. Brown/APL; (m) Corel; (b) Getty Images. 38: (t) Austin J. Brown/APL; (b) Airsport Photo Library. 39: (t) Airsport Photo Library; (b) Corel. 40: Corel. 41: (t) Austin J. Brown/APL; (b) Corel. 42: Corel. 43: Corel. 44: (t) EADS/APL; (b) NASA. 45: (t)Airbus S.A.S.; (b) Austin J. Brown/APL. 46: Lockheed Martin Aeronautics Company